BOUNDARIES: The Guide to Overcome Sexual Misconception

Work Book

Revising Negative Cognition to Positive in CSC Sexual Issues

By

Dr. Wanda A. Rogers & Dr. Cynthia Miller & Walter L. Banks

BOUNDARIES: The Guide to Overcome Sexual Misconception

Work Book

Revising Cognition in CRC Sexual Issues: is available at special quantity discounts to use as premiums and sales promotions, or for use in corporate training programs. To place a bulk order, please contact

Dr. Wanda A. Rogers at wanroge@reconciliationoflife.org

Table of Contents

Introduction

Instructions for the Sexual Issues

The purpose of this course is to provide the student with information on appropriate behavior towards the opposite sex. It is very important that we are cognizant of what might be deemed inappropriate to others.

It is very possible that some of us might have already made mistakes in this area. This course is certainly not to condemn you or try to shame anyone, but rather it is to make us aware so that we might live the life that God has intended for us to live. We can learn from our mistakes because if was confess our sins to God, He will definitely forgive us.

Life gives us boundaries; boundaries as pertaining to the law, to God and to oneself.

It is the hope of this facilitator that the information provided be a tool to help one overcome past mistakes and utilize this information to assist in building a new future in the Lord.

Outline of the Course

This course first gives the Michigan Laws as it pertains to sexual behavior around other people. Next, we move into the scriptures for direction to help one move into a stronger relationship with God and then to better understand oneself. It is certainly the hope of Reconciliation Ministries that those that take part in this course are elevated into a place of overcoming and triumph.

In this course we will learn the biblical application and simplified meaning of 2Corinthians 10:5 casting down every imagination, and every high thing that exalts itself against the knowledge of God and bringing in captivity every thought to the obedience of Christ. Wherefore, we will learn to change negative thinking into positive reaction (Reversed Positive Reaction Theory).

Boundaries

What is Sexual Harassment

The EEOC has defined sexual harassment in its guidelines as:
Unwelcome sexual advances, requests for sexual favors, and other verbal or physical conduct of a sexual nature when:

☐☐☐Submission to such conduct is made either explicitly or implicitly a term or condition of an individual's employment, or

☐☐☐Submission to or rejection of such conduct by an individual is used as a basis for employment decisions affecting such individual, or

☐☐☐Such conduct has the purpose or effect of unreasonably interfering with an individual's work performance or creating an intimidating, hostile, or offensive working environment.

Unwelcome Behavior is the critical word. Unwelcome does not mean "involuntary." A victim may consent or agree to certain conduct and actively participate in it even though it is offensive and objectionable. Therefore, sexual conduct is unwelcome whenever the person subjected to it considers it unwelcome. Whether the person in fact welcomed a request for a date, sex-oriented comment, or joke depends on all the circumstances.
Source: Preventing Sexual Harassment (BNA Communications, Inc.) SDC IP .73 1992 manual

Sexual harassment includes many things...

☐ ☐ ☐ Actual or attempted rape or sexual assault.

☐ ☐ ☐ Unwanted pressure for sexual favors.

☐ ☐ ☐ Unwanted deliberate touching, leaning over, cornering, or pinching.

☐ ☐ ☐ Unwanted sexual looks or gestures.

☐ ☐ ☐ Unwanted letters, telephone calls, or materials of a sexual nature
Unwanted pressure for dates.

☐ ☐ ☐ Unwanted sexual teasing, jokes, remarks, or questions.

☐ ☐ ☐ Referring to an adult as a girl, hunk, doll, babe, or honey.

☐ ☐ ☐ Whistling at someone.

☐ ☐ ☐ Cat calls.

☐ ☐ ☐ Sexual comments.

☐ ☐ ☐ Turning work discussions to sexual topics.

☐ ☐ ☐ Sexual innuendos or stories.

☐ ☐ ☐ Asking about sexual fantasies, preferences, or history.

☐ ☐ ☐ Personal questions about social or sexual life.

☐ ☐ ☐ Sexual comments about a person's clothing, anatomy, or looks.

☐ ☐ ☐ Kissing sounds, howling, and smacking lips.

☐ ☐ ☐ Telling lies or spreading rumors about a person's personal sex life.

☐ ☐ ☐ Neck massage.

☐ ☐ ☐ Touching an employee's clothing, hair, or body.

☐ ☐ ☐ Giving personal gifts.

☐ ☐ ☐ Hanging around a person.

☐ ☐ ☐ Hugging, kissing, patting, or stroking.

☐ ☐ ☐ Touching or rubbing oneself sexually around another person.

☐ ☐ ☐ Standing close or brushing up against a person.

☐ ☐ ☐ Looking a person up and down (elevator eyes).

☐ ☐ ☐ Staring at someone.

☐ ☐ ☐ Sexually suggestive signals.

☐ ☐ ☐ Facial expressions, winking, throwing kisses, or licking lips.

What is

Sexual Assault

To the victims of sexual assault, the various degrees can't take away the emotional and physical pain. But these specific degrees have been put in place in order to clearly define and prosecuted the perpetrators of these heinous acts. Each state has their own sexual assault degrees laws and penalties. Although there might be some slight variations in the details of codes and statutes there are some very clear cut common denominators about the degrees of sexual assault.

First Degree
First Degree Sexual Assault is considered a felony and the most serious of these types of offenses. This form of assault encompasses sexual intercourse or sexual contact without consent that results in pregnancy or bodily harm, or where a weapon or threat of a weapon was used or where one or more persons where involved in the assault through the use of threat or violence. Most rapes will fall under this degree of sexual assault. It carries the harshest of penalties which could mean up to forty years behind bars for each count.

Second Degree
Second Degree Sexual Assault is also a felony and pertains to sexual intercourse or sexual contact without consent as with First Degree Sexual Assault but other factors included in this degree concern the crime being committed against a person who is mentally impaired or physically disabled or who might be confined to a nursing home or even a prison. In some states, Second Degree Sexual Assault also applies to sexual contact without consent to a person who is under the age of twelve. Convictions of Second Degree Sexual Assault can land a person in jail for up to 25 years.

Third Degree
Third Degree Sexual Assault is considered a felony and concerns the same level of sexual intercourse or sexual contact without consent but deals with more specific assaults that might occur between members of the same household such as between husband and wife or between siblings. This can also include assaults that occur with minors between the ages of 12 and 18.

Fourth Degree
Not every state has a classification of Fourth Degree Sexual Assault but those that do consider this type of assault as a misdemeanor. Usually this involves sexual contact such as groping or exposing genitals but not necessarily intercourse. If sexual intercourse is involved with a Fourth Degree Sexual Assault, it is usually a sexual assault occurring between two minors. Fourth Degree Sexual Assault can carry a five-year jail term.

Sexual Assault is treated very seriously by the courts. Repeat offenders convicted of the same degree of sexual assault can fine their jail times doubled and tripled. Because the laws are so specific, it falls to the individual state's prosecutors to determine which degree of sexual assault to levy against the accused. In some cases, the degree of sexual assault can be lowered in a plea bargain arrangement. If a person is convicted of any degree of sexual assault, they will have to register with a national sexual offender's database.

What Is

Sexual Battery

Sexual Battery in Michigan refers to sex crimes not typically covered by rape statutes, such as unlawful sexual contact. Sexual battery is often characterized as sexual touching or penetration without consent of the person. The mere touching of another person for the purpose of sexual gratification qualifies as sexual battery. Penetration does not have to occur, unlike a rape charge. In Michigan, sexual battery is codified in the law under 4th degree criminal sexual conduct, defined as engaging in sexual contact with another person and if any of the following circumstances exist:

- Victim is at least 13 years of age but less than 16 years of age, and the actor is 5 or more years older than that other person.

- Force or coercion is used to accomplish the sexual contact.

- Knows or has reason to know that the victim is mentally incapable, mentally incapacitated, or physically helpless.

- Victim is related to the actor by blood or affinity to the third degree and the sexual contact occurs under circumstances not otherwise prohibited by this chapter. This does not apply if both persons are lawfully married to each other at the time of the alleged violation.

- The actor is a mental health professional and the sexual contact occurs during or within 2 years after the period in which the victim is his or her client or patient and not his or her spouse. The consent of the victim is not a defense to a prosecution under this subdivision. A prosecution under this subsection shall not be used as evidence that the victim is mentally incompetent.

Penalties for Sexual Battery in Michigan

The penalty for sexual battery classified under Criminal sexual conduct in the 4th degree is a misdemeanor punishable by imprisonment for not more than 2 years or a fine of not more than $500.00, or both.

Defense of a Sexual Battery in Michigan

The list of defenses for sexual battery in Michigan here is not exclusive but are the most common defenses used, which include:

- Consent (Sexual battery of a minor cannot use consent defense, nor can consent be used if the victim lacked the capacity to do)
- Insufficient evidence of incident (lack of physical evidence, lack of eyewitnesses)
- Improper police procedure (illegal questioning, sloppy evidence handling)
- False allegations/credibility issues ("he said, she said", jilted/angry partner)

Attempted Sexual Battery in Michigan

Attempted sexual battery occurs when the prosecution can prove that there was an intent by the defendant to place the victim in immediate threat and danger of sexual battery. If the prosecution can show a specific intent to commit a sexual battery, you can be found guilty. Common examples of this would be locking a victim in the bedroom for the purpose of sexual activity or drugging a victim with the intent of sexual contact.

When to Talk to a Lawyer

If you are charged with a sexual battery, it is critical to speak with a lawyer immediately. Getting a lawyer on your case immediately will assure that your rights are protected, that any evidence that can help you is preserved and the police and prosecution follow proper protocol. Sexual battery charges are serious crimes that have life altering consequences, and you should have an experienced criminal defense lawyer who can help your defense.

At this point, we will move into God's Word for help in this matter.

Leviticus 18:6-24 - King James Version (KJV)

[6] None of you shall approach to any that is near of kin to him, to uncover their nakedness: I am the LORD.

[7] The nakedness of thy father, or the nakedness of thy mother, shalt thou not uncover: she is thy mother; thou shalt not uncover her nakedness.

[8] The nakedness of thy father's wife shalt thou not uncover: it is thy father's nakedness.

[9] The nakedness of thy sister, the daughter of thy father, or daughter of thy mother, whether she be born at home, or born abroad, even their nakedness thou shalt not uncover.

[10] The nakedness of thy son's daughter, or of thy daughter's daughter, even their nakedness thou shalt not uncover: for theirs is thine own nakedness.

[11] The nakedness of thy father's wife's daughter, begotten of thy father, she is thy sister, thou shalt not uncover her nakedness.

[12] Thou shalt not uncover the nakedness of thy father's sister: she is thy father's near kinswoman.

[13] Thou shalt not uncover the nakedness of thy mother's sister: for she is thy mother's near kinswoman.

[14] Thou shalt not uncover the nakedness of thy father's brother, thou shalt not approach to his wife: she is thine aunt.

[15] Thou shalt not uncover the nakedness of thy daughter in law: she is thy son's wife; thou shalt not uncover her nakedness.

[16] Thou shalt not uncover the nakedness of thy brother's wife: it is thy brother's nakedness.

[17] Thou shalt not uncover the nakedness of a woman and her daughter, neither shalt thou take her son's daughter, or her daughter's daughter, to uncover her nakedness; for they are her near kinswomen: it is wickedness.

[18] Neither shalt thou take a wife to her sister, to vex her, to uncover her nakedness, beside the other in her life time.

[19] Also thou shalt not approach unto a woman to uncover her nakedness, as long as she is put apart for her uncleanness.

[20] Moreover thou shalt not lie carnally with thy neighbour's wife, to defile thyself with her.

[21] And thou shalt not let any of thy seed pass through the fire to Molech, neither shalt thou profane the name of thy God: I am the LORD.

[22] Thou shalt not lie with mankind, as with womankind: it is abomination.

[23] Neither shalt thou lie with any beast to defile thyself therewith: neither shall any woman stand before a beast to lie down thereto: it is confusion.

[24] Defile not ye yourselves in any of these things: for in all these the nations are defiled which I cast out before you:

Old Testament Sexual Encounters of the People of God

Noah: Three Son's Ham's Mocking:

Genesis 19:30-36 - King James Version (KJV)

[18] And the sons of Noah, that went forth of the ark, were Shem, and Ham, and Japheth: and Ham is the father of Canaan.

[19] These are the three sons of Noah: and of them was the whole earth overspread.

[20] And Noah began to be an husbandman, and he planted a vineyard:

[21] And he drank of the wine, and was drunken; and he was uncovered within his tent.

[22] And Ham, the father of Canaan, saw the nakedness of his father, and told his two brethren without.

[23] And Shem and Japheth took a garment, and laid it upon both their shoulders, and went backward, and covered the nakedness of their father; and their faces were backward, and they saw not their father's nakedness.

[24] And Noah awoke from his wine, and knew what his younger son had done unto him.

[25] And he said, Cursed be Canaan; a servant of servants shall he be unto his brethren.

[26] And he said, Blessed be the LORD God of Shem; and Canaan shall be his servant.

[27] God shall enlarge Japheth, and he shall dwell in the tents of Shem; and Canaan shall be his servant.

Contemplating the story:

We understand Noah's son Ham's descendants were cursed who are the Canaanites, Egyptians, Philistines, Hittites, and Amorites. We also know the whole Canaanite nation that knew God, but turned more wicked. The Bible tells us the other two sons were blessed. Shem's descendants are the: Hebrews, Chaldeans, Assyrians, Persians, and Syrian nations, and Japheth's descendants are the: Greeks, Thracians, and Scythians.

We see from the actions of the two older sons in this story that it is not good to look upon the nakedness of family members as previously read in Leviticus 18:6-24. We must understand the consequences behind these types of actions.

Complete the worksheet that follows.

Here we will pull out the negatives in the story:	Here we reverse the negative into: Positive Reaction
Example: And he drank of the wine, and was drunken.	Noah drank of the wine but only a small amount and did not become drunken.

Lot: The Sin of His Two Daughters

Genesis 19:30-36 - King James Version (KJV)

[30] And Lot went up out of Zoar, and dwelt in the mountain, and his two daughters with him; for he feared to dwell in Zoar: and he dwelt in a cave, he and his two daughters.
[31] And the firstborn said unto the younger, Our father is old, and there is not a man in the earth to come in unto us after the manner of all the earth:
[32] Come, let us make our father drink wine, and we will lie with him, that we may preserve seed of our father.
[33] And they made their father drink wine that night: and the firstborn went in, and lay with her father; and he perceived not when she lay down, nor when she arose.
[34] And it came to pass on the morrow, that the firstborn said unto the younger, Behold, I lay yesternight with my father: let us make him drink wine this night also; and go thou in, and lie with him, that we may preserve seed of our father.
[35] And they made their father drink wine that night also: and the younger arose, and lay with him; and he perceived not when she lay down, nor when she arose.
[36] Thus were both the daughters of Lot with child by their father.

Contemplating the story:

If you have not read the whole story or the generation of Lot go back and read it in Genesis. Nevertheless, now we want to talk about the consequences that came from the action of Lot's daughters and how that consequence or the actions of the daughters could have been reversed into a positive reaction for Lot's whole family. Describe in your own knowledge and in your own thoughts and words about the story.

Here we will pull out the negatives in the story:	Here we will reverse the negative into positive reaction:

Abraham: Affairs with Hagar and Ishmael

Genesis 16 - King James Version (KJV)

16 Now Sarai Abram's wife bare him no children: and she had an handmaid, an Egyptian, whose name was Hagar.

[2] And Sarai said unto Abram, Behold now, the LORD hath restrained me from bearing: I pray thee, go in unto my maid; it may be that I may obtain children by her. And Abram hearkened to the voice of Sarai.
[3] And Sarai Abram's wife took Hagar her maid the Egyptian, after Abram had dwelt ten years in the land of Canaan, and gave her to her husband Abram to be his wife.
[4] And he went in unto Hagar, and she conceived: and when she saw that she had conceived, her mistress was despised in her eyes.
[5] And Sarai said unto Abram, My wrong be upon thee: I have given my maid into thy bosom; and when she saw that she had conceived, I was despised in her eyes: the LORD judge between me and thee.
[6] But Abram said unto Sarai, Behold, thy maid is in thine hand; do to her as it pleaseth thee. And when Sarai dealt hardly with her, she fled from her face.

And Sarah saw the son of Hagar the Egyptian, which she had born unto Abraham, mocking.

[10] Wherefore she said unto Abraham, Cast out this bondwoman and her son: for the son of this bondwoman shall not be heir with my son, even with Isaac. [11] And the thing was very grievous in Abraham's sight because of his son. [12] And God said unto Abraham, Let it not be grievous in thy sight because of the lad, and because of thy bondwoman; in all that Sarah hath said unto thee, hearken unto her voice; for in Isaac shall thy seed be called. [13] And also of the son of the bondwoman will I make a nation, because he is thy seed.

[14] And Abraham rose up early in the morning, and took bread, and a bottle of water, and gave it unto Hagar, putting it on her shoulder, and the child, and sent her away: and she departed, and wandered in the wilderness of Beersheba. [15] And the water was spent in the bottle, and she cast the child under one of the shrubs. [16] And she went, and sat her down over against him a good way off, as it were a bow shot: for she said, Let me not see the death of the child. And she sat over against him, and lift up her voice, and wept.

[17] And God heard the voice of the lad; and the angel of God called to Hagar out of heaven, and said unto her, What aileth thee, Hagar? fear not; for God hath heard the voice of the lad where he is.

[18] Arise, lift up the lad, and hold him in thine hand; for I will make him a great nation.

[19] And God opened her eyes, and she saw a well of water; and she went, and filled the bottle with water, and gave the lad drink.

Here we will pull out the negatives in the story:	Here we will reverse the negative into positive reaction:

Judah: Impregnates his Daughter-in-law, Tamar

Genesis 38:12-26 - King James Version (KJV)

[12] And in process of time the daughter of Shuah Judah's wife died; and Judah was comforted, and went up unto his sheepshearers to Timnath, he and his friend Hirah the Adullamite.

[13] And it was told Tamar, saying, Behold thy father in law goeth up to Timnath to shear his sheep.

[14] And she put her widow's garments off from her, and covered her with a vail, and wrapped herself, and sat in an open place, which is by the way to Timnath; for she saw that Shelah was grown, and she was not given unto him to wife.

[15] When Judah saw her, he thought her to be an harlot; because she had covered her face.

[16] And he turned unto her by the way, and said, Go to, I pray thee, let me come in unto thee; (for he knew not that she was his daughter in law.) And she said, What wilt thou give me, that thou mayest come in unto me?

[17] And he said, I will send thee a kid from the flock. And she said, Wilt thou give me a pledge, till thou send it?

[18] And he said, What pledge shall I give thee? And she said, Thy signet, and thy bracelets, and thy staff that is in thine hand. And he gave it her, and came in unto her, and she conceived by him.

[19] And she arose, and went away, and laid by her vail from her, and put on the garments of her widowhood.

[20] And Judah sent the kid by the hand of his friend the Adullamite, to receive his pledge from the woman's hand: but he found her not.

[21] Then he asked the men of that place, saying, Where is the harlot, that was openly by the way side? And they said, There was no harlot in this place.

[22] And he returned to Judah, and said, I cannot find her; and also the men of the place said, that there was no harlot in this place.

[23] And Judah said, Let her take it to her, lest we be shamed: behold, I sent this kid, and thou hast not found her.

[24] And it came to pass about three months after, that it was told Judah, saying, Tamar thy daughter in law hath played the harlot; and also, behold, she is with child by whoredom. And Judah said, Bring her forth, and let her be burnt.

[25] When she was brought forth, she sent to her father in law, saying, By the man, whose these are, am I with child: and she said, Discern, I pray thee, whose are these, the signet, and bracelets, and staff.

[26] And Judah acknowledged them, and said, She hath been more righteous than I; because that I gave her not to Shelah my son. And he knew her again no more.

Here we will pull out the negatives in the story:	Here we will reverse the negative into positive reaction:

Samson: Delilah's Betrayal

Judges 16:1-20 - King James Version (KJV)

16 Then went Samson to Gaza, and saw there an harlot, and went in unto her. [2] And it was told the Gazites, saying, Samson is come hither. And they compassed him in, and laid wait for him all night in the gate of the city, and were quiet all the night, saying, In the morning, when it is day, we shall kill him. [3] And Samson lay till midnight, and arose at midnight, and took the doors of the gate of the city, and the two posts, and went away with them, bar and all, and put them upon his shoulders, and carried them up to the top of an hill that is before Hebron. [4] And it came to pass afterward, that he loved a woman in the valley of Sorek, whose name was Delilah.

[5] And the lords of the Philistines came up unto her, and said unto her, Entice him, and see wherein his great strength lieth, and by what means we may prevail against him, that we may bind him to afflict him; and we will give thee every one of us eleven hundred pieces of silver. [6] And Delilah said to Samson, Tell me, I pray thee, wherein thy great strength lieth, and wherewith thou mightest be bound to afflict thee. [7] And Samson said unto her, If they bind me with seven green withs that were never dried, then shall I be weak, and be as another man. [8] Then the lords of the Philistines brought up to her seven green withs which had not been dried, and she bound him with them. [9] Now there were men lying in wait, abiding with her in the chamber. And she said unto him, The Philistines be upon thee, Samson. And he brake the withs, as a thread of tow is broken when it toucheth the fire. So his strength was not known. [10] And Delilah said unto Samson, Behold, thou hast mocked me, and told me lies: now tell me, I pray thee, wherewith thou mightest be bound. [11] And he said unto her, If they bind me fast with new ropes that never were occupied, then shall I be weak, and be as another man. [12] Delilah therefore took new ropes, and bound him therewith, and said unto him, The Philistines be upon thee, Samson. And there were liers in wait abiding in the chamber. And he brake them from off his arms like a thread. [13] And Delilah said unto Samson, Hitherto thou hast mocked me, and told me lies: tell me wherewith thou mightest be bound. And he said unto her, If thou weavest the seven locks of my head with the web. [14] And she fastened it with the pin, and said unto him, The Philistines be upon thee, Samson. And he awaked out of his sleep, and went away with the pin of the beam, and with the web. [15] And she said unto him, How canst thou say, I love thee, when thine heart is not with me? thou hast mocked me these three times, and hast not told me wherein thy great strength lieth. [16] And it came to pass, when she pressed him daily with her words, and urged him, so that his soul was vexed unto death; [17] That he told her all his heart, and said unto her, There hath not come a razor upon mine head; for I have been a Nazarite unto God from my mother's womb: if I be shaven, then my strength will go from me, and I shall become weak, and be like any other man. [18] And when Delilah saw that he had told her all his heart, she sent and called for the lords of the Philistines, saying, Come up this once, for he hath shewed me all his heart. Then the lords of the Philistines came up unto her, and brought money in their hand. [19] And she made him sleep upon her knees; and she called for a man, and she caused him to shave off the seven locks of his head; and she began to afflict him, and his strength went from him. [20] And she said, The Philistines be upon thee, Samson. And he awoke out of his sleep, and said, I will go out as at other times before, and shake myself. And he wist not that the LORD was departed from him.

Here we will pull out the negatives in the story:	Here we will reverse the negative into positive reaction:

David: Sleeps with Bath-Sheba

2 Samuel 11 - King James Version (KJV)

And it came to pass, after the year was expired, at the time when kings go forth to battle, that David sent Joab, and his servants with him, and all Israel; and they destroyed the children of Ammon, and besieged Rabbah. But David tarried still at Jerusalem.

[2] And it came to pass in an eveningtide, that David arose from off his bed, and walked upon the roof of the king's house: and from the roof he saw a woman washing herself; and the woman was very beautiful to look upon.

[3] And David sent and enquired after the woman. And one said, Is not this Bathsheba, the daughter of Eliam, the wife of Uriah the Hittite?

[4] And David sent messengers, and took her; and she came in unto him, and he lay with her; for she was purified from her uncleanness: and she returned unto her house.

[5] And the woman conceived, and sent and told David, and said, I am with child.

[6] And David sent to Joab, saying, Send me Uriah the Hittite. And Joab sent Uriah to David.

[7] And when Uriah was come unto him, David demanded of him how Joab did, and how the people did, and how the war prospered.

[8] And David said to Uriah, Go down to thy house, and wash thy feet. And Uriah departed out of the king's house, and there followed him a mess of meat from the king.

[9] But Uriah slept at the door of the king's house with all the servants of his lord, and went not down to his house.

[10] And when they had told David, saying, Uriah went not down unto his house, David said unto Uriah, Camest thou not from thy journey? why then didst thou not go down unto thine house?

[11] And Uriah said unto David, The ark, and Israel, and Judah, abide in tents; and my lord Joab, and the servants of my lord, are encamped in the open fields; shall I then go into mine house, to eat and to drink, and to lie with my wife? as thou livest, and as thy soul liveth, I will not do this thing.

[12] And David said to Uriah, Tarry here to day also, and to morrow I will let thee depart. So Uriah abode in Jerusalem that day, and the morrow.

[13] And when David had called him, he did eat and drink before him; and he made him drunk: and at even he went out to lie on his bed with the servants of his lord, but went not down to his house.

[14] And it came to pass in the morning, that David wrote a letter to Joab, and sent it by the hand of Uriah.

[15] And he wrote in the letter, saying, Set ye Uriah in the forefront of the hottest battle, and retire ye from him, that he may be smitten, and die.

[16] And it came to pass, when Joab observed the city, that he assigned Uriah unto a place where he knew that valiant men were.

[17] And the men of the city went out, and fought with Joab: and there fell some of the people of the servants of David; and Uriah the Hittite died also.

[18] Then Joab sent and told David all the things concerning the war;

[19] And charged the messenger, saying, When thou hast made an end of telling the matters of the war unto the king,

[20] And if so be that the king's wrath arise, and he say unto thee, Wherefore approached ye so nigh unto the city when ye did fight? knew ye not that they would shoot from the wall?

[21] Who smote Abimelech the son of Jerubbesheth? did not a woman cast a piece of a millstone upon him from the wall, that he died in Thebez? why went ye nigh the wall? then say thou, Thy servant Uriah the Hittite is dead also.

[22] So the messenger went, and came and shewed David all that Joab had sent him for.

[23] And the messenger said unto David, Surely the men prevailed against us, and came out unto us into the field, and we were upon them even unto the entering of the gate.

[24] And the shooters shot from off the wall upon thy servants; and some of the king's servants be dead, and thy servant Uriah the Hittite is dead also.

[25] Then David said unto the messenger, Thus shalt thou say unto Joab, Let not this thing displease thee, for the sword devoureth one as well as another: make thy battle more strong against the city, and overthrow it: and encourage thou him.

[26] And when the wife of Uriah heard that Uriah her husband was dead, she mourned for her husband.

[27] And when the mourning was past, David sent and fetched her to his house, and she became his wife, and bare him a son. But the thing that David had done displeased the LORD.

Samuel 12 - King James Version (KJV)

And the LORD sent Nathan unto David. And he came unto him, and said unto him, There were two men in one city; the one rich, and the other poor.

[2] The rich man had exceeding many flocks and herds:

[3] But the poor man had nothing, save one little ewe lamb, which he had bought and nourished up: and it grew up together with him, and with his children; it did eat of his own meat, and drank of his own cup, and lay in his bosom, and was unto him as a daughter.

[4] And there came a traveller unto the rich man, and he spared to take of his own flock and of his own herd, to dress for the wayfaring man that was come unto him; but took the poor man's lamb, and dressed it for the man that was come to him.

[5] And David's anger was greatly kindled against the man; and he said to Nathan, As the LORD liveth, the man that hath done this thing shall surely die:

[6] And he shall restore the lamb fourfold, because he did this thing, and because he had no pity.

[7] And Nathan said to David, Thou art the man. Thus saith the LORD God of Israel, I anointed thee king over Israel, and I delivered thee out of the hand of Saul;

[8] And I gave thee thy master's house, and thy master's wives into thy bosom, and gave thee the house of Israel and of Judah; and if that had been too little, I would moreover have given unto thee such and such things.

[9] Wherefore hast thou despised the commandment of the LORD, to do evil in his sight? thou hast killed Uriah the Hittite with the sword, and hast taken his wife to be thy wife, and hast slain him with the sword of the children of Ammon.

[10] Now therefore the sword shall never depart from thine house; because thou hast despised me, and hast taken the wife of Uriah the Hittite to be thy wife.

[11] Thus saith the LORD, Behold, I will raise up evil against thee out of thine own house, and I will take thy wives before thine eyes, and give them unto thy neighbour, and he shall lie with thy wives in the sight of this sun.

[12] For thou didst it secretly: but I will do this thing before all Israel, and before the sun.

[13] And David said unto Nathan, I have sinned against the LORD. And Nathan said unto David, The LORD also hath put away thy sin; thou shalt not die.

[14] Howbeit, because by this deed thou hast given great occasion to the enemies of the LORD to blaspheme, the child also that is born unto thee shall surely die.

[15] And Nathan departed unto his house. And the LORD struck the child that Uriah's wife bare unto David, and it was very sick.

[16] David therefore besought God for the child; and David fasted, and went in, and lay all night upon the earth.

[17] And the elders of his house arose, and went to him, to raise him up from the earth: but he would not, neither did he eat bread with them.

[18] And it came to pass on the seventh day, that the child died. And the servants of David feared to tell him that the child was dead: for they said, Behold, while the child was yet alive, we spake unto him, and he would not hearken unto our voice: how will he then vex himself, if we tell him that the child is dead?

[19] But when David saw that his servants whispered, David perceived that the child was dead: therefore David said unto his servants, Is the child dead? And they said, He is dead.

[20] Then David arose from the earth, and washed, and anointed himself, and changed his apparel, and came into the house of the LORD, and worshipped: then he came to his own house; and when he required, they set bread before him, and he did eat.

[21] Then said his servants unto him, What thing is this that thou hast done? thou didst fast and weep for the child, while it was alive; but when the child was dead, thou didst rise and eat bread.

[22] And he said, While the child was yet alive, I fasted and wept: for I said, Who can tell whether GOD will be gracious to me, that the child may live?

[23] But now he is dead, wherefore should I fast? can I bring him back again? I shall go to him, but he shall not return to me.

Here we will pull out the negatives in the story:	Here we will reverse the negative into positive reaction:

Absalom: David's Son Rapes Tamar, His Sister:

2 Samuel 13- King James Version (KJV)

And it came to pass after this, that Absalom the son of David had a fair sister, whose name was Tamar; and Amnon the son of David loved her.

² And Amnon was so vexed, that he fell sick for his sister Tamar; for she was a virgin; and Amnon thought it hard for him to do anything to her.

³ But Amnon had a friend, whose name was Jonadab, the son of Shimeah David's brother: and Jonadab was a very subtil man.

⁴ And he said unto him, Why art thou, being the king's son, lean from day to day? Wilt thou not tell me? And Amnon said unto him, I love Tamar, my brother Absalom's sister.

⁵ And Jonadab said unto him, Lay thee down on thy bed, and make thyself sick: and when thy father cometh to see thee, say unto him, I pray thee, let my sister Tamar come, and give me meat, and dress the meat in my sight, that I may see it, and eat it at her hand.

⁶ So Amnon lay down, and made himself sick: and when the king was come to see him, Amnon said unto the king, I pray thee, let Tamar my sister come, and make me a couple of cakes in my sight, that I may eat at her hand.

⁷ Then David sent home to Tamar, saying, Go now to thy brother Amnon's house, and dress him meat.

⁸ So Tamar went to her brother Amnon's house; and he was laid down. And she took flour, and kneaded it, and made cakes in his sight, and did bake the cakes.

⁹ And she took a pan, and poured them out before him; but he refused to eat. And Amnon said, Have out all men from me. And they went out every man from him.

¹⁰ And Amnon said unto Tamar, Bring the meat into the chamber, that I may eat of thine hand. And Tamar took the cakes which she had made, and brought them into the chamber to Amnon her brother.

¹¹ And when she had brought them unto him to eat, he took hold of her, and said unto her, Come lie with me, my sister.

¹² And she answered him, Nay, my brother, do not force me; for no such thing ought to be done in Israel: do not thou this folly.

¹³ And I, whither shall I cause my shame to go? And as for thee, thou shalt be as one of the fools in Israel. Now therefore, I pray thee, speak unto the king; for he will not withhold me from thee.

¹⁴ Howbeit he would not hearken unto her voice: but, being stronger than she, forced her, and lay with her.

¹⁵ Then Amnon hated her exceedingly; so that the hatred wherewith he hated her was greater than the love wherewith he had loved her. And Amnon said unto her, Arise, be gone.

¹⁶ And she said unto him, There is no cause: this evil in sending me away is greater than the other that thou didst unto me. But he would not hearken unto her.

¹⁷ Then he called his servant that ministered unto him, and said, Put now this woman out from me, and bolt the door after her.

¹⁸ And she had a garment of divers colours upon her: for with such robes were the king's daughters that were virgins appareled. Then his servant brought her out, and bolted the door after her.

¹⁹ And Tamar put ashes on her head, and rent her garment of divers colours that was on her, and laid her hand on her head, and went on crying.

²⁰ And Absalom her brother said unto her, Hath Amnon thy brother been with thee? But hold now thy peace, my sister: he is thy brother; regard not this thing. So Tamar remained desolate in her brother Absalom's house.

²¹ But when king David heard of all these things, he was very wroth.

²² And Absalom spake unto his brother Amnon neither good nor bad: for Absalom hated Amnon, because he had forced his sister Tamar.

²³ And it came to pass after two full years, that Absalom had sheepshearers in Baalhazor, which is beside Ephraim: and Absalom invited all the king's sons.

²⁴ And Absalom came to the king, and said, Behold now, thy servant hath sheepshearers; let the king, I beseech thee, and his servants go with thy servant.

²⁵ And the king said to Absalom, Nay, my son, let us not all now go, lest we be chargeable unto thee. And he pressed him: howbeit he would not go, but blessed him.

²⁶ Then said Absalom, If not, I pray thee, let my brother Amnon go with us. And the king said unto him, Why should he go with thee?

²⁷ But Absalom pressed him, that he let Amnon and all the king's sons go with him.

²⁸ Now Absalom had commanded his servants, saying, Mark ye now when Amnon's heart is merry with wine, and when I say unto you, Smite Amnon; then kill him, fear not: have not I commanded you? Be courageous, and be valiant.

²⁹ And the servants of Absalom did unto Amnon as Absalom had commanded. Then all the king's sons arose, and every man gat him up upon his mule, and fled.

³⁰ And it came to pass, while they were in the way, that tidings came to David, saying, Absalom hath slain all the king's sons, and there is not one of them left.

[31] Then the king arose, and tare his garments, and lay on the earth; and all his servants stood by with their clothes rent.

[32] And Jonadab, the son of Shimeah David's brother, answered and said, Let not my lord suppose that they have slain all the young men the king's sons; for Amnon only is dead: for by the appointment of Absalom this hath been determined from the day that he forced his sister Tamar.

[33] Now therefore let not my lord the king take the thing to his heart, to think that all the king's sons are dead: for Amnon only is dead.

[34] But Absalom fled. And the young man that kept the watch lifted up his eyes, and looked, and, behold, there came much people by the way of the hill side behind him.

[35] And Jonadab said unto the king, Behold, the king's sons come: as thy servant said, so it is.

[36] And it came to pass, as soon as he had made an end of speaking, that, behold, the king's sons came, and lifted up their voice and wept: and the king also and all his servants wept very sore.

[37] But Absalom fled, and went to Talmai, the son of Ammihud, king of Geshur. And David mourned for his son every day.

[38] So Absalom fled, and went to Geshur, and was there three years.

[39] And the soul of king David longed to go forth unto Absalom: for he was comforted concerning Amnon, seeing he was dead.

Here we will pull out the negatives in the story:	Here we will reverse the negative into positive reaction:

Hosea's Wayward Wife

Hosea 1 - King James Version (KJV)

1 The word of the LORD that came unto Hosea, the son of Beeri, in the days of Uzziah, Jotham, Ahaz, and Hezekiah, kings of Judah, and in the days of Jeroboam the son of Joash, king of Israel.

2 The beginning of the word of the LORD by Hosea. And the LORD said to Hosea, Go, take unto thee a wife of whoredoms and children of whoredoms: for the land hath committed great whoredom, departing from the LORD.
3 So he went and took Gomer the daughter of Diblaim; which conceived, and bare him a son.
4 And the LORD said unto him, Call his name Jezreel; for yet a little while, and I will avenge the blood of Jezreel upon the house of Jehu, and will cause to cease the kingdom of the house of Israel.
5 And it shall come to pass at that day, that I will break the bow of Israel, in the valley of Jezreel.
6 And she conceived again, and bare a daughter. And God said unto him, Call her name Loruhamah: for I will no more have mercy upon the house of Israel; but I will utterly take them away.
7 But I will have mercy upon the house of Judah, and will save them by the LORD their God, and will not save them by bow, nor by sword, nor by battle, by horses, nor by horsemen.
8 Now when she had weaned Loruhamah, she conceived, and bare a son.
9 Then said God, Call his name Loammi: for ye are not my people, and I will not be your God.
10 Yet the number of the children of Israel shall be as the sand of the sea, which cannot be measured nor numbered; and it shall come to pass, that in the place where it was said unto them, Ye are not my people, there it shall be said unto them, Ye are the sons of the living God.
11 Then shall the children of Judah and the children of Israel be gathered together, and appoint themselves one head, and they shall come up out of the land: for great shall be the day of Jezreel.

Here we will pull out the negatives in the story:	Here we will reverse the negative into positive reaction:
	.

New Testament Story of Sexual Issues

Paul on Sexual Sin

1 Corinthians 5:1-5 - King James Version (KJV)

It is reported commonly that there is fornication among you, and such fornication as is not so much as named among the Gentiles, that one should have his father's wife.

[2] And ye are puffed up, and have not rather mourned, that he that hath done this deed might be taken away from among you.
[3] For I verily, as absent in body, but present in spirit, have judged already, as though I were present, concerning him that hath so done this deed,
[4] In the name of our Lord Jesus Christ, when ye are gathered together, and my spirit, with the power of our Lord Jesus Christ,
[5] To deliver such an one unto Satan for the destruction of the flesh, that the spirit may be saved in the day of the Lord Jesus.

1 Corinthians 7: 1-9 - King James Version (KJV)

Now concerning the things whereof ye wrote unto me: It is good for a man not to touch a woman.

[2] Nevertheless, to avoid fornication, let every man have his own wife, and let every woman have her own husband.
[3] Let the husband render unto the wife due benevolence: and likewise also the wife unto the husband.
[4] The wife hath not power of her own body, but the husband: and likewise also the husband hath not power of his own body, but the wife.
[5] Defraud ye not one the other, except it be with consent for a time, that ye may give yourselves to fasting and prayer; and come together again, that Satan tempt you not for your incontinency.
[6] But I speak this by permission, and not of commandment.
[7] For I would that all men were even as I myself. But every man hath his proper gift of God, one after this manner, and another after that.
[8] I say therefore to the unmarried and widows, it is good for them if they abide even as I.
[9] But if they cannot contain, let them marry: for it is better to marry than to burn.

Here we will pull out the negatives in the story:	Here we will reverse the negative into positive reaction:

Questions and answers (multiple choice) - Choose the best answer to your understanding:

1. We know that Noah became drunk, but what does the bible tell us about this type of action?
   A. Drinking is okay; so drink much as you want.
   B. Getting drunk is a cool thing to do.
   C. Wine is a mocker, strong drink is raging: and whosoever is deceived thereby is not wise.

2. When Lot's daughters decided that they would go in and sleep with their father, they were committing what type of sin?
   A. Incest
   B. Lust
   C. Adultery

3. In our time, Abraham sleeping with Sarah's handmaid, Hannah, would have been a type of what type of sin?
   A. Disrespectful
   B. Willful
   C. Adultery

4. In the story of Judah and his daughter-in-law, he committed two types of sin. Which two types of sin was it?
   A. Incest and fornication
   B. Adultery and lascivious
   C. Heresy and strife

5. What was the primary cause of Samson losing his life in the story?
   A. Lust
   B. Love
   C. Betrayal

6. What caused David to want to sleep with Uriah the Hittite's wife.
   A. Pride
   B. Lust
   C. Love

7. What caused Amnon to want to sleep with Tamar, his sister, and what kind of sin did he commit?
   A. Care and compassion
   B. Hate and love
   C. Lust and incest

8. What type of sin did Hosea's wife commit against Hosea and what were her eyes full of?
   A. Fornication and lust
   B. Lust and pride
   C. Adultery and lust

9. How many sins did the man commit by having his father's wife as Paul tells us in the story in 1Corinthians 5 and 7? Circle all the correct answers.
   A. Incest
   B. Fornication
   C. Adultery
   D. Pride
   E. Lust
   F. All of the above

The Person with Problems in the Area of Sexual Issues - The Modern-Day Leper

Leprosy is a disease that was spoken of in the Bible. The term "leprosy" (including leper, lepers, leprosy, leprous) occurs 68 times in the Bible—55 times in the Old Testament and 13 times in the New Testament. In the Old Testament, the instances of leprosy most likely meant a variety of infectious skin diseases, and even mold and mildew on clothing and walls. The precise meaning of the leprosy in both the Old and New Testaments is still in dispute, but it probably includes the modern Hansen's disease (especially in the New Testament) and infectious skin diseases. Many have thought leprosy to be a disease of the skin. It is better classified, however, as a disease of the nervous system because the leprosy bacterium attacks the nerves. Leprosy's agent *M. leprae* is a rod-shaped bacterium related to the tuberculosis bacterium. Leprosy is spread by multiple skin contacts, as well as by droplets from the upper respiratory tracts, such as nasal secretions that are transmitted from person to person. The Lepers were forced to live apart from society because the disease was highly contagious. They were not supposed to co-mingle with the rest of society.

Why this discussion on leprosy?

Because in some instances, the individual with sexual issues has been declared unworthy of ever being a productive part of society, forgiven for past transgressions, or to have access to the redemptive power of Jesus Christ. This class seeks to help all involved move from condemnation, self condemnation and judgment to a place of living in the total resurrection power of the Lord Jesus Christ!

> *2 Corinthians 5:17, "Therefore if any man be in Christ, he is a new creature: old things are passed away; behold, all things are become new."*

The Importance of Forgiving Yourself Through the Love of God

When you look inside, you hate yourself, you could kick yourself over and over for your past failures and choices. You've come to Jesus and repented, but you haven't really accepted the truth about what Jesus has done for you yet. You still feel ashamed and guilty over your past and you keep holding it against yourself.

The way you see yourself is not an accurate picture of what Christ has done for you. It is basically denying the work that Jesus accomplished for you on the cross! If your sins are forgiven, then you need to see yourself as separated from your sins...but know that the enemy will try diligently to remind you of your past and continue to beat you up over sins that were supposed to be nailed to the cross. You are wrapped up in guilt and condemnation my friend... and you NEED to forgive yourself. You can go through deliverance, but if you don't forgive yourself for the mistakes you've made, you won't experience the breakthrough that you need to be totally set free.

If you don't see yourself as a new creature in Christ, you will be hindered and held back from freely and confidently living out who you really are in Christ! You will be hesitant and feel unworthy to approach your Heavenly Father, because you feel you're a failure and unworthy. This is why it is vital for your conscience to be cleansed of dead works (your past failures).

Hebrews 9:14, "How much more shall the blood of Christ, who through the eternal Spirit offered himself without spot to God, purge your conscience from dead works to serve the living God?"

Failing to forgive yourself will put blinders on your spiritual eyesight quickly. It will cause you to see things through the eyes of guilt, shame and condemnation. It will ruin your faith, and cause you to go blind spiritually.

2 Peter 1:9, "But he that lacketh these things is blind, and cannot see afar off, and hath forgotten that he was purged from his old sins."

God's Word tells us that Jesus purged (that is, removed) our sin (Hebrews 1:3, "...when he had by himself purged our sins..."), but if we fail to forgive ourselves, we are in essence, calling God's Word a lie! We are saying, "I hate myself because I did that sin... I won't forgive myself of it!" when God's Word tells us that the sin has been PURGED or REMOVED from us... who are we to say that it is still part of our past? We are in essence, calling God's Word a LIE!

This is where we discuss how they feel about themselves. Those that are unable to talk about it are most likely in need of special prayer.

Controlling Our Thoughts

How can we do that? Do you mean that God expects us to take control of our thoughts? Yes, He does. We have the help of this scripture.

Finally, brothers, whatever is true, whatever is noble, whatever is right, whatever is pure, whatever is lovely, whatever is admirable--if anything is excellent or praiseworthy--think about such things. (Philippians 4:8)

Let us carefully examine this Scripture by dissecting it precept by precept.

Discuss the meaning of each of these words.

- Whatever is **true**-

    A. What do you feel absolutely certain of?

    B. Does your life represent the truth you believe in?

- Whatever is **noble** –

    A. What does being noble mean to you?

    B. Do you consider yourself to be of noble character?

    C. Is there anyone you consider to be noble?

- Whatever is **right** –

    A. How do you determine right and wrong?

    B. Where does your moral judgment originate? Is it your upbringing? Is it your relationship with God?

- Whatever is **pure**-

    A. What does it mean to be pure?

    B. Can you see purity in a person?

    C. Would you describe yourself as pure?

- Whatever is **lovely?**

    A. Describe something that is lovely?

    B. Is there anything lovely in your life?

- Whatever is **admirable** –

    A. Define admiration.

    B. Is there a person or situation that you admire? Share with the class.

- Whatever is **praiseworthy** –

    A. Describe a situation that you found to be praiseworthy or excellent.

    B. Speak about the goodness of the situation.

    C. If it is person, talk about that person.

    D. What did you learn from that situation?

Now, let all of these words germinate in your thinking. Concentrate on these words and purposefully try to use these words in your thinking every day.

2 Corinthians 10:5

Casting down imaginations, and every high thing that exalteth itself against the knowledge of God, and bringing into captivity every thought to the obedience of Christ;

Paul wrote that *we do not war according to the flesh* (2 Cor. 10:3-5). Our warfare is not of this world; it is *divinely powerful for the destruction of fortresses*. That is, if you have a stronghold, which is a deeply embedded sinful habitual pattern, you can pull it down and destroy it by appropriating the powerful spiritual warfare that is ours in Christ. We destroy "*vain imaginations*" (KJV), *speculations and every lofty things raised up against the knowledge of God*, by casting down any thought that does not line up with the Word of God or what we know of the Son of God.

We take *the thought captive to the obedience of Christ*. That is, we march the thought that we captured before we acted upon it, and present our captive thought to our Commander in Chief, Jesus Christ. We ask Him to crucify the thought and by faith thank Him for doing so. Then we continue our walk of faith. Great truth. Now how does it work?

Thought - "I am such a bad Christian that God could never really love me." Truth-That thought does not line up with the Word of God. I John 4:10 says, *"In this is love,not that we loved God, but that He loved us and sent His Son to be the propitiation for our sins."* (See, this is why you must know the Word of God! How else will you recognize the vain imaginations that are lifted up against the knowledge of God?)

Test - Can you capture the thought or do you get some kind of perverted pleasure from denigrating yourself? Do put-downs come easily? Has your self-worth been so debased that you really believe the lies the enemy is shooting your way? Can you capture the thought before you act upon it (giving into depression or self-loathing) and turn to the Lord, marching the thought at gunpoint (mentally) to your Commander in Chief and asking Him to crucify the thought.

Triumph - Yeah! You have taken your thought captive to the obedience of Christ, cast down the lies of the enemy, crucified self and exalted Christ in your life. God gets all the glory because our weapons are not of this world, but they are "other-worldly!" Sister-you rock!

This process works for any lie of the enemy ("You are stupid", "You are worthless", "You are a bad mother" etc.) or any stronghold (anger, jealously, lust, envy, etc.) that has built a giant honking strong tower in your psyche. This, sisters, is how you pull it down...brick by brick...you are delivered as you repeat the process so many times that it becomes as natural to you as breathing. When you are successful, you put your foot on the neck of your enemy and he is forced to admit that Jesus is Lord!

Therefore, we must put on the helmet of salvation (to guard our thought life) lest we allow the enemy to find a chink in our armor and exploit it or lest we allow a sinful and habitual pattern to remain unchecked and develop into a stronghold. So, my beloved internets, memorize Scriptures that will be useful when the enemy comes against you to your specific weakness and point of vulnerability. Hold forth the shield of faith, draw the sword of the spirit and fight the good fight of faith.

Sexual Misconception

In the present day we are a sexualized world; most of the stuff having to do with our daily lives are sexual. So, we also must be aware of the less talked about sexual misconduct, because whether it be rape, sexual harassment, proper sexual touching or unwanted sexual advice, we all can learn from the wrongdoings of one another. I have long battled with sexual impurity. My mother, being black, used to say that I was mannish, but there really is the question when is too much not enough, like having a crush on your teacher, but what about looking under her dress or skirt. That's just a child being young, but immature thoughts lead to improper actions. As a young child my thoughts ran rapid until my first sexual experience at the age of 10. Until then my thoughts would wander, thinking about what was on the inside of a woman's body, truly thinking. I think those early thoughts were then what prompted my actions. My first real sexual encounter happened at the age of 12. After that I was rapidly becoming addicted to this thing known as sex, because at the age of 14 I could seduce a much older woman that was to become my son's mother. She taught me things that, until I met her, had eluded me. So when I finally could please a woman, and receive from a woman, my thoughts would still travel. However, I was now experiencing a greater range of sexual encounters. My family consists of a lot of women with 15% men and 85% women. It is just that young ladies, sex, drugs, and immaturity doesn't add up. I can think about a couple of incidences where I gave in to temptation and also tempted some family members to engage in incest. Pleasure sometimes overrides logic. I was beginning to think as if it was not wrong if we both wanted to do it because we are both consenting. **Now that I think about it sometimes, one wrong does seem right, but when you flip the situation and look at it from all perspectives, I know that when you are doing right you are okay, but sometimes while doing wrong we make ourselves think that it's okay if we don't get caught.** Look at it like this, if your mother could see your actions, would you still do it? If not, then it's wrong. Females can't always be the one to blame because certain situations don't involve them until we make it their problem. **There are men that believe they are entitled to a woman whether it be though force or choice.** Most rapists didn't start off that way; they later became that. I am labeled as a sexual predator, and I didn't have sex with my victim; but, the intent was there, so I understand what it means to get a label. Recently, I was talking to a young mother of one we met and got to know each other along the way. She found out that I was a sexual offender, and, being the mother of one young son, she was scolded by her family for endangering her son's safety by going out with a sexual offender. Never mind that my victim was a young lady; she was 17 years old. We spoke, and she quietly ended the relationship because she felt she didn't want to have to hide nothing from her aunt and family. Now I know once I was convicted of my crime people would look at me wrong or in a different light. As I sit writing this statement I am reminded that, no, I don't hide what got me in prison, but neither do I publicly shout to the world that I am a sex offender. Being in prison there are a lot of guy's that say you shouldn't have to take a woman by force, and messing with children is a death sentence. My mother wanted me to write something on the issue of sexual misconduct, so I finally gave her the gift she wanted for Christmas. It isn't always easy to talk openly, but it is necessary because people tend to sweep things under the rug if the world doesn't know about it. It isn't right how many females have been raped but haven't told anyone. So I know we must talk about this issue now, and I have opened the door, so that others can share the issues with the public.

Questions to help guild your cognitive thinking: Reversed Positive Reaction Therapy (RPRT) turns negative into positives helping develop a person's thoughts, actions, and behaviors productively. As we keep our sexual boundaries in the forefront of the mind we can do as God ask us to:

*Casting down imaginations, and **every** high thing that exalteth itself against the knowledge of God, and **bring**ing into captivity **every thought** to the obedience of Christ;* (2Corinthians 10:5)

God also tell us: *But I say unto you, That whosoever looketh on a woman to lust after her hath committed adultery with her already in his heart (*Matthew 5:28).

1. What was your most inappropriate sexual thought? How can you reverse this thought, so it becomes a positive thought?

2. Have you ever done something you felt bad about sexually?

3. Could you have went to prison for something you had done sexually but never got caught?

4. In relationship, do you feel sexual tension because of a past issue in your life? Past sexual encounters can cause intense sexual desires. Rape, child molestation, and seeing others sexually assaulted.

5. How have you stepped on other's sexual boundaries?

6. What happens when you are not committed before sexual intercourse?

7. Did you have an adult teach you about healthy sex association growing up? If not, do you feel it would have helped you control your sexual desires more?

8. How do you set boundaries for yourself and respect other's boundaries?

Self-Respect and Respecting Other's Boundaries

Reverse Positive Reaction Theory (RPRT)

There's a male 21years old and a female 15 year of age. In the beginning the young woman told the male that she was 18 years of age, and they both agreed to have sex in a video, but when the time presented itself the young lady became fearful and reluctant to go through with the sex tape. Under pressure by the male, she tried talking her way out providing her state identification with her true age. The male became enraged and forced her to have sex with him on video. He then sent it to a multitude of friends in their community. The young woman's parents discovered what had transpired, and charges were brought against the male.

Now allow me to implicate the RPRT. In the first instance, this theory should have been used to end the CSC case. The male could of, at that moment the young woman advised him of her true age and providing her identification card, STOPPED instead of becoming enraged. He should have stopped and thought about the situation, taking an alternative route, by allowing the young lady to leave. He should have thought of the consequences that would follow his actions. Forcing sex on the minor, taking the time to think rather than acting, is vital to a person's future. Think about the life of someone else. Positive mental thinking will prevent a horrible outcome of most situations dealing with life in this type of predicament.

The Answers to the Questions Old Testament and New Testament

1. C. Proverbs 20:1 Wine is a mocker, strong drink is raging: and whosoever is deceived thereby is not wise.

2. A. Leviticus 18:6-7 [6] None of you shall approach to any that is near of kin to him, to uncover their nakedness: I am the LORD. [7] The nakedness of thy father, or the nakedness of thy mother, shalt thou not uncover: she is thy mother; thou shalt not uncover her nakedness.

3. C. Exodus 20: 14 and Hebrews 13:4 [14] Thou shalt not commit adultery. [4] Marriage is honourable in all, and the bed undefiled: but whoremongers and adulterers God will judge.

4. A. Leviticus 18:15 and Corinthians 6:9 [15] Thou shalt not uncover the nakedness of thy daughter in law: she is thy son's wife; thou shalt not uncover her nakedness. [9] Know ye not that the unrighteous shall not inherit the kingdom of God? Be not deceived: neither fornicators, nor idolaters, nor adulterers, nor effeminate, nor abusers of themselves with mankind.

5. A. Proverbs 5:3-11 [3] For the lips of a strange woman drop as an honeycomb, and her mouth is smoother than oil: [4] But her end is bitter as wormwood, sharp as a two-edged sword. [5] Her feet go down to death; her steps take hold on hell. [6] Lest thou shouldest ponder the path of life, her ways are moveable, that thou canst not know them. [7] Hear me now therefore, O ye children, and depart not from the words of my mouth. [8] Remove thy way far from her, and come not nigh the door of her house: [9] Lest thou give thine honour unto others, and thy years unto the cruel: [10] Lest strangers be filled with thy wealth; and thy labours be in the house of a stranger; [11] And thou mourn at the last, when thy flesh and thy body are consumed,

6. B. James 1:14 [14] But every man is tempted, when he is drawn away of his own lust, and enticed.

7. C. Matthew 5:28 and Leviticus 18:9 [28] But I say unto you, That whosoever looketh on a woman to lust after her hath committed adultery with her already in his heart. [14] The nakedness of thy sister, the daughter of thy father, or daughter of thy mother, whether she be born at home, or born abroad, even their nakedness thou shalt not uncover.

8. C. 2Peter 2:14 1John 2:16 [14] Having eyes full of adultery, and that cannot cease from sin; beguiling unstable souls: an heart they have exercised with covetous practices; cursed children: [16] For all that is in the world, the lust of the flesh, and the lust of the eyes, and the pride of life, is not of the Father, but is of the world.

9. All of them are corrected.

Discussion Notes

_____
_____
_____
_____
_____
_____
_____
_____
_____
_____
_____
_____
_____
_____
_____
_____
_____
_____
_____
_____
_____
_____
_____
_____
_____
_____
_____
_____
_____
_____
_____
_____

Discussion Notes

_____
_____
_____
_____
_____
_____
_____
_____
_____
_____
_____
_____
_____
_____
_____
_____
_____
_____
_____
_____
_____
_____
_____
_____
_____
_____
_____
_____
_____
_____

Discussion Notes

_____
_____
_____
_____
_____
_____
_____
_____
_____
_____
_____
_____
_____
_____
_____
_____
_____
_____
_____
_____
_____
_____
_____
_____
_____
_____
_____
_____
_____
_____
_____

Discussion Notes

_____
_____
_____
_____
_____
_____
_____
_____
_____
_____
_____
_____
_____
_____
_____
_____
_____
_____
_____
_____
_____
_____
_____
_____
_____
_____
_____
_____
_____
_____
_____

Discussion Notes

_____

_____

_____

_____

_____

_____

_____

_____

_____

_____

_____

_____

_____

_____

_____

_____

_____

_____

_____

_____

_____

_____

_____

_____

_____

_____

_____

_____

_____

_____

www.ingramcontent.com/pod-product-compliance
Lightning Source LLC
Chambersburg PA
CBHW080940030426

42339CB00008B/467